Time Management

Proven Methods For Increasing Productivity, Reducing Stress, And Improving Work-life Balance

(Tips And Techniques For Optimal Productivity)

Pierre Atkinson

TABLE OF CONTENT

Chapter 1: Tips For Managing Your Time Better...... 1

Chapter 2: Put An Exercise In 17

Chapter 3: Commence The Day Properly 21

Chapter 5: How To Create A Schedule For Effective Time Management 38

Chapter 6: How Adults Interpret Time 46

Chapter 7: Our Most Valuable Currency Must Be Time. 54

Chapter 8: Strategies For Managing Time For High School Students 61

Chapter 9: Understanding Your Current Productivity 69

Chapter 10: Consider The Consequences Of Procrastination 77

Chapter 11: Compile A List Of Your Daily Duties 86

Chapter 12: Time Administration And Its Significance 96

Chapter 13: Determine Which Portion Of The Elephant Appears Most Appetizing 101

Chapter 14: Consider Why You Are Delaying Actions 115

Chapter 16: Tips For Successful Time Management 125

Chapter 1: Tips For Managing Your Time Better

Be your own greatest cheerleader: After becoming aware of your desires and determining your goals, the next step is to encourage yourself to work toward achieving those goals.

Ultimately, if you do not believe you are capable of accomplishing your goals, there is no way you will succeed.Visualize yourself achieving your goals. Specify the reward that awaits you at the conclusion of your journey. And remember the importance of self-confidence at all times.

Plan ahead: Planning is the initial step on the path to attaining your goals through effective time management. Planning is the first action to take if your objectives are the endpoint you are working toward.

Without a plan, you have a greater chance of getting confused, and thus a greater chance of failure. Plans reveal what must be done and when it must be accomplished.To create your strategies, you must conduct a second analysis of your goals. Create a list of the activities and procedures that will aid you in attaining your goals, and eliminate anything you deem to be a distraction.

resolve what to do: You won't get very far if you don't resolve which path to take before you reach the crossroads. You may not even reach this point. Nevertheless, since inaction and procrastination are ineffective, the best course of action would be to summon courage and make a decision.If you can effectively manage your time, you won't feel rushed and you won't feel as much strain when making decisions; as a result, you'll be able to make better life decisions in general.

This is a difficult query, especially if you prefer to deliberate for a long time before making decisions and if you frequently do not know what to do next. However, the strategy you outlined earlier in the day may come in beneficial at this point.Asking yourself, "What is the very first step I need to take to get to the next point in my plan?" is a good question to ask when you are uncertain about which decision to make.

Question your decisions: You've made some decisions along the path to accomplishing your goals; however, are you certain that they were the best ones? After all, making the wrong decision could cause you to deviate from your objectives and squander valuable time.Just consider the following:

Will this decision bring me closer to my goals?

Where do the threats reside?

Are the benefits of selecting this option greater than the possible drawbacks?

How committed am I to my selected path?

You will save yourself a great deal of time that you would later spend rectifying the consequences of your poor decisions if you do not proceed with what you had previously decided. If the answers you receive are unsatisfactory, you should not proceed with your original plan.

Establish priorities and organize materials: If you don't prioritize and focus on your work, you won't be able to determine which of these tasks are the most important and urgent for achieving your goals. Numerous prioritization strategies are available, so you have a choice between the ones listed below. In addition, there is a technique known as the Pomodoro technique that is an effective method for controlling inveterate procrastinators.

Scheduling blocks of time to focus on multiple initiatives simultaneously may be a straightforward tactic that yields impressive results. This strategy is most useful for regaining control of one's schedule and enhancing the work-life balance quality of one's life.

Give priority to the most important tasks: If you allow your mind to wander to less important tasks, you will rarely finish what you have started. After prioritizing and organizing what is essential, the next step is to focus on your priorities.

Several potential courses of action:

Except for the tab you are currently working on, you should dismiss all other tabs in your browser when you are at work.

Put down your smartphone and focus your full attention on the task at hand.

Turn off your computer and give your undivided attention to the people who matter most to you at this time, whether they are coworkers or family members.If you concentrate on perfecting one task at a time, you will be able to reflect back on your time and feel satisfied that it was well spent.

Maintain a log of the time you expend on each assignment:Keeping track of the amount of time spent on each of your daily responsibilities must be a crucial component of effective time management, correct?In essence, absolutely.Due to our frequent time constraints, it is imperative that we maximize the time we do have. Utilizing time-tracking software is quite beneficial in this situation.How?

Keeping account of time has many benefits, but the following are a few:

Increases production through increased motivation.

Encourages enhanced organization and prioritization, which is especially advantageous for remote teams.

Promotes healthful behaviors while discouraging unhealthy ones.

Provides focus while also facilitating in maintaining schedule adherence.

Improves your comprehension of your time management skills

Allows you to have a greater understanding of your limitations.

Helps you avoid time and resource waste.

Avoid working lengthy hours: Consider the following scenario:

You are currently juggling numerous responsibilities.

You are tempted to sacrifice some of your time in order to finish everything.

You decide to put in extended hours or work on the weekends for the sake of your success, even though you know it will only be temporary.

However, the quantity of work that must be completed continues to increase, and despite your best efforts, you are never able to meet all of the deadlines.

You continue to engage in this behavior despite the fact that there is no escape, as you have already been a part of a vicious cycle.

You begin to experience health issues, are unable to spend time with your friends and family, and become depressed as a result.

If you identify with any of these symptoms, you are likely overworked. In addition, it indicates that you are close to exhaustion; therefore, you must take a break and recalibrate your priorities. Even though it is easy to let our obligations dominate our lives, this does not mean that we must. To manage the mountain of work that has been heaped upon your shoulders, you must reevaluate your priorities and devise a strategy. You can get started by:

The first stage, recognizing that you are working longer than necessary, is frequently the most challenging.

Mastering the ability to decline additional obligations and responsibilities when necessary.

When you have a lot on your schedule or the deadline is approaching, you should delegate projects and responsibilities.

Calling for assistance whenever you believe it is necessary.

Stress, in its most fundamental form, is an ineffective and counterproductive factor that leads nowhere.Even if you spend all of your time fretting about the outcomes of your actions and decisions, your efforts will yield the same results.If there is nothing you can do to affect the outcome of the situation, you should not be concerned about it. Developing healthful coping mechanisms for the daily stress you experience should be your number one priority. This is especially essential if you wish to safeguard your health and prevent burnout.What does stress management involve?

Preventing one's problems from invading one's mind when one is not actively attempting to resolve them.

Spending time with cherished ones, whether family or friends.

I am attempting a distinct activity.

Having a wonderful time and a great deal of laughter.

Time management and tension management are frequently intertwined and should be addressed concurrently.When you feel in control of your time, you experience less tension, and when you experience less stress, you may live a healthier and more relaxed lifestyle.When you reduce the amount of stress in your life, you will not only feel more capable of resolving life's challenges swiftly, but you will also save time in the process.

In today's fast-paced society, when you're exhorted to be quick (but successful) and aggressive (yet faultless), patience is rarely regarded as a virtue worth cultivating.You will squander more time if you delay making decisions, but if you try to get from A to B as quickly as possible, you will make decisions that are not in your best interest.If you practice patience on occasion, you can demonstrate your commitment to attaining success and reduce the likelihood that you will make mistakes along the way.

Consider the reasons behind your impatience before anything else. Is the item you're awaiting of such vital importance that you need to keep it in mind at all times and spend all of your time sitting around?There is a strong likelihood that it is not.Alternately, you could focus your attention and effort on a different aspect of your life; after all, aimlessly waiting for something over which you have no control or ability to expedite is the most inefficient use of time.

Learn to manage challenging situations and obstacles: Problems and obstacles stand in the way of the straight path to your objectives.If you do not learn to overcome them, you will be unable to proceed. And if you attempt to avoid them without addressing them, they will likely mess you up further down the road.There is a solution to every problem; do not leave any stone untouched in your search for solutions.

Additionally, you can attempt the following:

Analyze the issue from every angle.

Call your family and acquaintances for assistance.

Deal with your issues as soon as feasible.

Determine the best solutions to each problem with perseverance.

Ask your teammates for their opinions and suggestions.

Recognize when it is time to abandon a project.

Cooperate and maintain open lines of communication: You may have greater control over a situation if you manage it on your own, but that does not mean you should or even that you can. When you communicate and collaborate with your colleagues and coworkers, you can accomplish more in the same amount of time because there are more of you working on a task.

The same remains true for your close friends and family members; you could save a great deal of time throughout your life if you simply allowed them to assist you, either directly or by providing you with advice and guidance. When confronted with a problem that you cannot solve on your own, you should seek assistance. Be forthright, employ simple language, and make it your mission to explain (if it is not already clear) why something is significant to you. It is normal and acceptable to believe that you need the assistance of others to live a better life.

Chapter 2: Put An Exercise In

The relationship between the body and the mind has been demonstrated. As a business proprietor, it is essential that you take sufficient exercise breaks each day. You will lose motivation if you do not take care of your physique.

You do not need to devote a great deal of time to exercise, purchase an expensive gym membership, or employ an expensive personal trainer. Start by taking a vigorous 30-minute walk in the morning, during your lunch break, or in the evening. Once you've established a regular walking regimen, consider

extending the length of your treks or scheduling two daily walks.

It may take some time for you to determine what works best for you, but it is essential that you get started immediately. You will begin to feel better almost immediately.

Consider keeping weights at your workstation so that you can exercise for brief periods throughout the day. Many business owners maintain a television at work so they can watch CNN or NBC while exercising.

BE ORDINATE

Organization is crucial for sustaining motivation. If you are constantly searching for misplaced documents or consistently responding to customer and business partner communications late, it is difficult to feel motivated about your work. Without sufficient organization, you will lose motivation, and your business will suffer.

Numerous individuals find it difficult to become organized. If this describes you, there is no disgrace in seeking assistance. You can enlist the help of a friend or family member to clean up your mess and eliminate the clutter, or you can employ a professional to do it for you. It is remarkable how important this one step is to having your home-based business back on track. Implement company systems that can help you streamline operations to keep things moving.

Maintaining the mechanisms you've established and staying on course will be your greatest obstacles. This is a problem that many business owners face on a daily basis, but if you successfully implement these strategies, you'll have more time to focus on other crucial aspects of your home-based business.

Chapter 3: Commence The Day Properly

More Organization

For many individuals, the dawn is frequently tumultuous. You slumber excessively and awaken far too late. Then the true hustle begins: showering, brushing one's teeth, sending the children to school, eating a quick breakfast or even checking one's email, and then hopping into one's car to confront the wonderful daily traffic as if dawn had ambushed one. Upon reading this, you are likely already anxious. A morning ritual gives you more control over your day and provides structure to your life.

Less Anxiety

After regaining control of your morning, you will encounter fewer interruptions. You decide how your morning will unfold and at what pace. Unexpected events no longer cause you to be rushed, which means you won't arrive at work irritated before the start of the day. You will experience less stress if you commence each day with greater vigor and a more positive attitude.

Physical and Emotional Connection

Emotional well-being can be significantly impacted by physical health. With all of the illness, we do not typically wear a smile or act excessively ebullient.

Moreover, how we perceive we are organizing our day may affect our mental health. We may become easily overwhelmed, agitated, despondent, and frustrated if we are constantly rushing to make the next meeting, always falling behind, or feeling lost in a sea of tasks.

It is understandable that we might begin to feel hopeless and as if we will never catch up if this trend persists. In our daily lives, a sense of serenity and self-assurance can help us maintain positive mental health and become significantly more resilient in stressful situations.

When we are overburdened and under duress, our emotions can quickly begin to manifest in our interactions with important people in our lives. How often have you returned home after a long, stressful day to lash out at a family member or close friend? This could be accomplished through venting, expressing wrath, or isolating oneself from caring individuals. As we establish a morning ritual that allows us to develop confidence, creativity, and vitality, we may observe that our interactions become more robust, connected, and pleasant.

Productivity

The morning regimen allows us to set the tone for the day, allowing us to take control of our schedules rather than being controlled by them. If we begin each day with a clean slate, we may be able to concentrate better on what is in front of us, determine where to prioritize our time, and ultimately increase our productivity.

Productivity relates to the amount of effort and intent we put into our jobs, as well as the quantity of work we accomplish. Ten unfinished tasks at the end of the day are vastly different from completing six tasks and being immensely proud of your effort. When we are constantly responding to additional responsibilities, pressures, or the needs of others, it may be challenging to establish priorities and continue.

Confidence

Being self-confident requires more than simply stating, "I like myself." Genuine confidence is bolstered by past encounters. The term "identity" refers to our confidence in our abilities to achieve goals and complete duties. Ego, which is an evaluation of our feelings about our personalities, is less effective than self-efficacy in fostering confidence and resilience.

Walking through our day, observing ourselves complete tasks, and feeling a sense of accomplishment may bolster our sense of self-assurance. A daily schedule can assist with prioritization, time management, and productivity. These will almost surely increase your sense of self-efficacy.

Peace

Stress can have psychological, physical, professional, and personal effects on us. Feeling incapable of completing responsibilities or perpetually falling behind is stressful. When our sense of self is inadequate, we may engage in negative self-talk and become anxious and agitated.

A reliable, consistent morning routine can enable us to engage in purposeful meditation and/or prayer, resulting in greater feelings of calmness throughout the day. Feeling productive outside can contribute to a more tranquil evening, a restful night's sleep, and an energizing start to the following day.

Feel in Command

When you have a large number of responsibilities, you are constantly rushing. Instead of you dominating the day, the day begins to dominate you. A morning ritual may only consume a small portion of your day, but it may be the first step in regaining control.

Chapter 4: The Act of Balancing Work, Family, and Private Time

Occasionally, the tensions between family life and daily work obligations can be overwhelming. Adaptability to work demands may be hindered, for instance, by personal issues such as relationship difficulties or concerns regarding dependent care. Alternately, as work demands increase, less energy and time are available for family, friends, and personal pursuits, which may negatively impact the quality of your personal life.

Regardless of the issues or circumstances, an imbalance between work and personal life may result in increased (negative) stress, acrimony, or disappointment (with professional life, personal life, or both). Finding solutions to reduce conflicts between work and family is an ongoing process.

prohibitive of constructing a harmonious and stable existence. This can start with determining what truly matters.

To begin, we may need to:

Define what we genuinely want out of life. Determine what motivates our decisions. Establish and achieve goals that will enhance the congruence in our lives and strengthen our relationships.

This begins with your perspective, which is not something you discover. YOU are responsible for creating balance (by making difficult decisions).

The most severe problem is that most people believe they have no or few options. However, this is not precisely true.

Remember that the balance between work and leisure is largely determined by your decisions, and that this is the source of your stress. By agreeing to take on additional work when you do not have the capacity or by failing to delegate tasks that could be delegated, you increase your own burden.

Change your mindset:

Recognize that you can make errors. For example, if you are working on a project, recognize that it is unlikely that your work will be flawless, particularly at first. In addition, you may choose to begin by writing down some initial responses before evaluating your work at the end to determine whether any corrections are required.

Confront your anxieties. Identify your fears and strive to overcome them if you are delaying something due to fear. You may convince yourself, for instance, that your goal is to simply get something written down and that you can always edit it later if you're concerned that it won't be good enough.

Increase your self-assurance. Self-efficacy is the conviction that you are capable of taking the measures necessary to achieve your goals. This will reduce your procrastination and any associated issues, such as anxiety. Consider your ability to effectively implement the numerous study and assignment-completion strategies available, and attempt to identify them, in order to increase your self-efficacy.

Remember that anti-procrastination techniques are most effective when they are tailored to the specific causes of procrastination. Try employing methods that will make it feel more manageable, such as dividing it down into a series of small tasks, if you have put off working on your thesis because it seems too daunting.

In addition, keep in mind that to completely overcome your procrastination, you may first need to address any underlying causes, such as ADHD, melancholy, or sleep deprivation.

If professional assistance is required, obtain it.

Learn to prepare

To keep track of your activities and timetable, you must schedule your time and record it. It appears that everything has a place and is in its location. Determine the time of day during which you are most productive and schedule your most important tasks at that time.

Utilize the planning instrument that best suites your needs. There are numerous scheduling applications that can alert you of approaching appointments or deadlines. However, some individuals continue to prefer paper planners. Choose what is optimal for you, then adhere to it. Here are some time management guidelines to remember:

- If you use both a paper planner and planning software or an electronic planner, ensure that the two are always in harmony.

- Daily review of your itinerary or planner is required.

- Always carry your planner with you.

Prepare yourself.

A place for everything and a workstation devoid of clutter are essential. The highest priority is decluttering. If you do not require it, sell it, donate it, or dispose of it. After decluttering, it's possible to implement an organization system. Being organized provides the greatest opportunity for enhancing productivity.

Eliminate distractions

After addressing all issues on your end, such as evaluating how you use your time, planning, intelligently allocating your time, and organizing yourself, you will need to address the distractions caused by your immediate surroundings. This category encompasses both electronic and interpersonal diversions.

When evaluating how you spent your time, you made a list of all the interruptions you experienced throughout the day. You can uninstall or conceal apps that are electronic distractions if they are not required for your job. Close your email and silence your phone when you are working diligently. Whenever possible, avoid being around people who will be a distraction.

Your productivity will increase if you effectively manage your time. Using the aforementioned tips, you will be able to better manage your time and focus on the most important duties, thereby increasing your productivity.

Chapter 5: How To Create A Schedule For Effective Time Management

Step 1: Determine the Available Time
Establishing the amount of time you will devote to your business should be the initial step.

The amount of time spent at work should reflect the structure of your job and your life goals.

For instance, if you are vying for a promotion, it may be prudent to put in additional time each day to demonstrate your dedication. On the other hand, if you desire to have ample time for extracurricular activities, you can choose to work only the allotted number of hours.

Step 2: Plan Crucial Steps
Next, list the actions you must take to complete the work successfully. These are frequently the standards by which you will be evaluated.

Ensure you have sufficient time to attend to the guidance, monitoring, and personal concerns of your team members if you manage people, for example. Give yourself time to communicate with your employer and other significant people in your life.

The following phase involves scheduling your top priorities.
Include high-priority, urgent tasks as well as maintenance tasks that cannot be neglected or outsourced on your to-do list.

Try to schedule them for the times of day when you are most productive; for example, some people are more productive in the morning, when they are most energized and effective, while others are more productive in the afternoon or evening, when they can focus better. Read our article "Is This a Morning Task?" to learn how to determine your optimal times of day.

Step 4: Make emergency preparations
Next, allocate additional time for handling emergencies and unforeseen circumstances. In general, the more unpredictable your endeavor, the more buffer time you will need. Experience will teach you how much leeway to provide. (If you do not plan for this time, crises will still arise, and you will be required to remain late to complete your task.)

Step 5: Schedule Discretionary Time
The remaining time on your schedule is "discretionary time," which can be used

to accomplish your priorities and goals. Examine your priority to-do list and personal goals, determine the amount of time required to complete them, and schedule time in your calendar.

Step 6: Evaluate Your Actions
If, by the time you reach step five, you discover that you have little to no free time, you should revisit stages two, three, and four to determine whether or not all of the duties you've entered are necessary. Certain duties may be delegated or completed in a more efficient manner.

Utilizing the leverage you can generate with your time is one of the most important ways to achieve success. You can complete more work by delegating tasks to others, outsourcing essential tasks, and automating as much of your work as feasible using technology. This will allow you to accomplish your goals.

If you find that you still have limited spare time, you may need to renegotiate your workload or seek assistance. Utilize your recently produced schedule as evidence of your numerous obligations. This demonstrates to your management that you are organized, which can make him or her more receptive to your proposal!

In this context, the term 'Character' refers to discipline. To make effective use of time, one must have developed a degree of self-control over his desires and be principled -- doing what needs to be done rather than what he or she feels like doing.

Especially if you operate remotely and are not directly supervised regarding your time management. You become fatigued, sleepy, and hungry, lose your motivation to work, and are even tempted to watch television and eat a snack to relax, and before you realize it, the day has been wasted.

Discipline is an indispensable instrument for meeting deadlines. You should learn to apply time constraints to yourself before others do so for you.

This will help you become a trustworthy coworker. You earn the reputation of someone who can be relied upon to complete outstanding work without missing deadlines.

Without a doubt, there will be unanticipated tasks that you must complete, either delegated to you by a superior or an imperative need that you did not anticipate or include on your to-do list but which requires your full attention. Therefore, I recommend that you make your daily to-do list flexible in order to accommodate such duties.

Still, many individuals mistake procrastination for adaptability. They focus on unanticipated emergencies at the expense of attaining their daily objectives. They are content with switching tasks and not making time to work on their predetermined goals, which will bring them closer to achieving their life objectives.

Flexibility requires the ability to attend to a crucial but unanticipated duty while also focusing on your daily objectives.

In such a scenario, you may run out of time and be unable to complete your written assignment in full. Therefore, you should begin with the most important and imperative task on your list, which is typically the task you will find most challenging to begin with, but which will give you the greatest sense of accomplishment and increase your productivity.

Start with these tasks, then move on to those that are important but less imperative, and so on, until you've completed everything on your list or you're left with something that requires less of your time and mental energy. These tasks can be delegated to a competent individual who can perform them effectively.

Rarely do you have the desire to put in the necessary effort to accomplish the success you desire. Move your feet to your workspace without a second thought to how exhausted you are (if you truly feel unwell, see a doctor), sit down, and begin working on your materials. The first few minutes are the most difficult, but after those few minutes, I'm confident you'll fall in love with your workflow.

Chapter 6: How Adults Interpret Time

As we progress through life pursuing this rodent race to do more in order to have more, time becomes the scarce commodity we no longer possess. Therefore, when we are young, we have all the time in the world to dream and aspire to become great persons one day. Yet as we mature, we realize that time no longer works in our favor throughout the majority of our daily lives.

Consider the treatment of scarce commodities and resources by humans. We are taught, in accordance with standard economic principles, that scarce resources must always be handled with the utmost 'sensitivity', as it is against the law to exploit resources when we are aware that they are running out. Therefore, we must treat them with the utmost care by creating situations and conditions that enable us to preserve them. Therefore, in cases of supply and demand, economics will increase the cost of restricted resources so that fewer parties can acquire them. Conversely, the opposite would be true regarding resources and commodities that are in abundance. With this analogy in mind and knowing how often we adults complain about not having enough time to do this or that, why do we not treat time as the genuinely valuable and scarce resource that it is and make the most of it?

As you can see, I have been in your position. You grow up with the desire to have everything. As soon as you graduate college and are ready to face the real world, all you can think about is working as hard as possible to cross the finish line as swiftly as possible and live the life of your dreams. You press yourself and keep going, but shortly after entering the race of life, certain realities become apparent. You suddenly notice that your milestones are getting further away, despite the fact that you're still running at the same pace you began with. However, you are driven and determined that nothing will deter you, so you press yourself even further and consider various strategies that could assist you in achieving your goals. Perhaps a better employment will suffice, or perhaps a second source of income will improve your quality of life. So you press yourself further, run faster, and observe the passage of time accelerate.

You are oblivious to the imbalance that your diligent work is causing in other areas of your life for which you can no longer find the time. We refer to this as spreading oneself thin —You're working too hard to be everywhere at once, which prevents you from giving each aspect of your life the attention it deserves. So, year after year, your persistent pursuit of achieving your dreams affects an additional aspect of your existence. You observe yourself developing poor habits consistent with disappointments, procrastination, lethargy, and ultimately a lack of concentration.

When we lack a profound and accurate comprehension of time and its value, we are unable to move past and overcome the daily imbalances and obstacles we face. While we may have a relentless desire to get up every morning and continue doing what we're doing, we lose sight of the true essence and significance of why we're doing what we're doing. Are you in the position you desire? Does the quality of your existence currently provide you with satisfaction and fulfillment? Once you realize that you are not where you want to be and are not living a balanced, fruitful, and satisfying life, you realize that the place in which you continue to invest your time is not producing the desired results. And yet, you wake up every day for months and years, sacrificing and devoting your entire existence to something that isn't even leading you to your desired destination.

When I realized my struggle, observed that I was exhausted, and reached a point where I felt I was no longer joyful and had lost the true meaning of life, I knew I had to make changes. I desired to transfer my attention to my true desires. I desired a satisfying balance in my life that would allow me to live my life as I wished without sacrificing another aspect of my life that is essential to me. I desired for my time to be more purposeful.

After conducting extensive research on how I could transform my life for the better, make my time valuable, and balance every aspect of my life, I began to experience positive self-transformation after making it my mission to understand and implement the techniques and principles that would guide me on this journey.

Like the majority of you, I had my share of humble beginnings marked by considerable struggle and loss. As I worked diligently to make a name for myself and made my way through life, I went through the typical stages that most millennials go through in wanting to have it all while still trying to find my own feet and niche in this life. But there came a time when I sensed that something needed to change about me and my entire existence. Despite having something to look forward to each morning, I was miserable, feeling void, and dissatisfied with the quality of life I was leading. I needed more answers, which prompted me to seek for the ones that would propel me on my journey of transformation.

Today, as I write this to you, I am a successful entrepreneur who has mastered the philosophy of time management. In my true definition of wealth, I believe I have it all because I have the abundance of serenity, freedom, and success that I've always desired due to the mindset I've adopted and practiced using everything that I'm about to share with you in this book.

Even though I am able to wake up each day with a heart of genuine appreciation and gratitude for the life I am able to afford myself today, I feel somewhat fortunate to be in a position where I can impart and share so much with you while having a solid and relatable foundation that knows and understands where you are right now. Because I have been in your shoes, everything that I will share with you is extremely personal and sentimental to me. And because of my current position and success, I am able to share with you my insights and personal experiences based on what I know works from my own personal experiences.

Chapter 7: Our Most Valuable Currency Must Be Time.

Have you ever been perplexed as to why your financial responsibilities and monthly expenditures continue to increase as you age? Well, it's a fact of life that new phases of your life will require you to invest money in order to get things done. For instance, even a decision as simple as deciding to be in a romantic relationship incurs costs, such as paying for dates, arranging occasional outdoor excursions, and not to mention the funds required to make daily calls and send texts. Imagine what your life will be like after you get married, have children, rent an apartment, and buy a car. These expenses just keep building up. Life and the cost of living are costly, and everything has a cost.

You are now confronted with all of these realities, and you must find a solution to your problems. Yes! A better-paying position should be the solution. Or perhaps a different source of income will suffice. Therefore, you labor harder and put in more hours in order to increase that source of income or obtain that new position. Now the workload has increased, and you have ultimately obtained the job or extra income. Consequently, you experience a brief period of happiness and optimism about the future because you appear to have regained control. However, in less than a month, you're already considering purchasing a new vehicle, obtaining more credit, or relocating to a better location. Eventually, you will be back at square one with a mountain of debt to manage and expenses that appear out of nowhere.

This is the financial rodent race I mentioned earlier. It is when you live from paycheck to paycheck, if not in overdraft and credit. You are the hamster in the wheel that continues running and running and running, getting faster and faster, but no matter how hard you try, you never receive the trite reward that should make the race worthwhile.

You devote so much time and effort to establishing your professional working career in order to ostensibly live the life you desire, without realizing that this is at the expense of other areas of your life. So you're trapped in this financial rat race, perpetually dissatisfied because other aspects of your life are suffering, and you never have time to pursue your desires.

Whether it's intentional or not, the majority of people tend to be a part of this rodent race. It originates from the belief that if one earns more money, they will be able to maintain their ever-increasingly extravagant lifestyle. Your education degree, for which you sacrificed and suffered for years, is now put to the test because it should yield you a high-paying job, allowing you to end your struggles. Unfortunately, at this point, you do not realize that this mentality is only the beginning of your problems, despite the fact that you believe you have reached the conclusion.

This is an undeniable fact that must never be disregarded. It is an independent force that enables us to spend in order to acquire better items in life. In essence, we receive money in order to expend it. This holds true even for those who save, as they ultimately do so in order to purchase something. You believe it is your right and should be justified because you deserve the best in life, "Especially when you work so hard." However, this is not the case.

Then, What Is My Point?

To get the most out of this book, you must first rid yourself of all outmoded ideas and conditioning. Be open to the need for change and willing to adopt new methods of thinking about time. Next, prioritize intentionally appreciating time, as it is the only currency that cannot be redeemed. In life, there will always be various distractions that will mislead you and cloud your judgment, ultimately wasting your time and the time of others to avoid focusing on what you should be focusing on, such as cultivating relationships and creating the most memorable experiences with the people who matter the most. So, you fall into the trap of constantly promising yourself that it is for you and those you care about, when in reality, no matter how quickly you run, you will never reach the cheese.

Learn to recognize time as your most valuable asset. By recognizing that the time you have is a luxury that you may not have previously appreciated, acquiring this knowledge enables you to see the potential that exists, as you can now see the time you have as a luxury that you may not have previously valued. In a summary, a greater appreciation for time corresponds to a greater utilization of it.

Chapter 8: Strategies For Managing Time For High School Students

Numerous high school students contend with exhaustion, interruptions, and poor time management. However, with coaching and some professional advice, you can assist them in achieving their full potential. They will benefit from developing time management skills in the classroom and in their future roles as parents, laborers, and leaders.

As a role model, you must establish a balance between offering assistance when needed and preventing excessive dependence. Your children will become outstanding students in no time if you strive to achieve this balance and provide them with the appropriate advice. The following are some techniques you can teach them:

Work During Productive Hours: Some pupils are early birds, while others are night owls, just as we all are. If a student appears exhausted every morning, studying prior to the start of class is likely to hinder their retention. The same can be said for children who awake each morning with a positive attitude. If they begin their homework late at night, they may not have enough energy to complete their assignments and learn from them.

Therefore, encourage afternoon-active students to begin their assignments after school dismisses. Ensure that they have study snacks and sufficient water to fuel their minds. Alternatively, children who rise earlier may have greater success studying on the bus or in the cafeteria during breakfast. Instruct them not to wait until the morning to complete all of their homework, even if they are exhausted after dinner.

Limit Distractions: It's no secret that social media is one of the greatest time-wasters for occupied students, but certain apps can help relieve tension. For instance, scrolling through animal videos on Instagram could help students reach their "happy place" during work breaks. In fact, 30% of young adults report that using social media in this manner reduces their tension and anxiety. However, you should still encourage students to reserve social media use for brief pauses between subjects.

Here are some additional techniques they can use to eliminate distractions:

Obtain an app that can block social media at predetermined times.

Put the phone on vibrate mode.

Turn off the phone until it is time for a respite.

Work in a room distinct from video games, televisions, and other forms of entertainment.

Eliminate Stressful Interactions: A student may frequently view or participate in content on social media that increases their stress, such as intense debates on emotive subjects. Logging into their accounts may cause more daily tension than they are aware of, resulting in emotional exhaustion. To get them to focus on their assignments, have a discussion about avoiding online toxicity.

Request that they limit their exposure to content on social media that makes them feel negatively. When students realize how much better they feel after logging out of their accounts, they may decide to limit their usage in their personal time as well.

Other methods of tension management include:

Discuss issues with a responsible adult.

Count to ten while concentrating on a joyful notion.

In a planner, schedule a specific amount of time for social media.

Create Time Blocks to encourage your students to consider more about time management. Using a planner to divide assignments into neat time segments, for instance, will aid in maintaining focus. You can also encourage them to do the following as they develop a reliable schedule:

Set regular intervals of 10 to 15 minutes duration.

Create sections for subjects and other endeavors.

Separate study time and homework time.

Create a list of avoidable procrastination behaviors.

Utilize distinct colored markers for each block type.

Establish Daily Routines: Designating specific study time will ensure that students remain on track with their coursework. In addition, students who struggle in particular subjects should work with a tutor or attend an instructor's after-school assignment help hours. Assist them in developing a schedule that accommodates any extracurricular activities in which they participate.

Other activities that can be accommodated in a planner may include:

A weekly event or activity, such as viewing their favorite television program.

designated supper and snack breaks.

Quick study breaks during which they can investigate a topic that interests them, such as a particular president or Greek architecture.

Chapter 9: Understanding Your Current Productivity

Consider the following factors that may have a significant impact on your business productivity:

What's Going on Right Now?

Starting the day without a strategy

If you commence the day without a plan of action, you're already doomed! You begin tardily and feel overwhelmed immediately. You then spend the remainder of the day in a defensive and crisis-oriented state of mind.

You may also find yourself responding hastily and arbitrarily to other people's problems and events and placing them above your own.

No equilibrium

There are seven important areas of life in which we must maintain equilibrium in order to be happy and successful:

Wellness - how your body feels and responds to outside stimuli

Responsibility and quality time spent with cherished ones

Financial - extent of fiscal obligations and revenue commitments

Intellectual - how external stimuli influence existence

Social - one's interactions with others

Professional - the methods you employ to further your profession

Spiritual - your connection with a higher power and other individuals

Each of these areas requires daily time for completion, although they may not all receive equal daily time. It's not essential to invest a great deal of time in every area, but it is essential to invest some time in every area. Our lives will be balanced and harmonious in the long term if we can devote sufficient time and effort to all aspects. However, neglecting any of these areas can rapidly destroy your chances for success.

When we neglect our own well-being, for instance, our loved ones and social life suffer. Similarly, when our financial resources are depleted, we are unable to fully concentrate on our professional objectives, career aspirations, and other crucial areas of concentration.

Untidy workplace

A cluttered workstation may result in a cluttered mind.

When essential customer-related business documents and information are missing, problems arise. These factors can lead to confusion, confusion, and more confusion, as well as lost sales and delayed invoicing. Studies have shown that workers with cluttered desks spend approximately one to two hours per day seeking for items and becoming distracted. This can result in a considerable quantity of weekly wasted time.

Weak recovery

Due to lack of sleep, many of his web entrepreneurs are unable to achieve their business objectives or see results. In relation to vital business functions, insufficient sleep can result in irrational decision making and poor judgment.

According to studies, nearly 75% of internet entrepreneurs suffer from sleep deprivation, which negatively impacts their enterprises. Being exhausted is neither beneficial nor productive for home-based work.

If entrepreneurs are not negatively affected by sleep deprivation, their quality of slumber will be poor. This indicates that when they do fall asleep, it is typically an irregular and restless sleep due to tension and other debilitating factors.

Network operators can be endangered and ultimately harmed by stressful days. The key to reducing stress and enhancing productivity is adequate rest and sleep.

Network administrators make a grave error when they take frequent and reasonable breaks. I feel as though I shouldn't or can't consider taking a respite because I lack the regimented or rigid schedule of the corporate world. Sometimes you feel that it is a waste of time. Not truthful. A sufficient amount of sleep is essential for daily success. Internet entrepreneurs frequently fail to take sufficient breaks because they believe they can produce superior results without them.

They believe that working nonstop will make them more successful and prolific, despite the fact that it does not produce more results or longer working hours.

Acquaint yourself with the letter N

Becoming comfortable with declining commitments that do not bring you closer to your objectives is a crucial step in developing better time management skills. Saying "no" to something that is not serving you or assisting you in achieving your goals frees up time for more essential activities, such as spending time with loved ones, getting in shape, or catching up on sleep.

If you find it difficult to say "no," recall a time when you gave in to duress and said "yes," only to feel regret later. Either you did the work reluctantly because you were overcommitted and lacked the time and resources to complete it, or you did not complete it at all. It is much easier to simply say no from the start, and doing so will allow you to focus on the things that truly matter.

minimizing disruptions as much as possible

Reducing interruptions may be interpreted as a form of refusal. Please explain what has caught your attention. Email? Texts? We're discussing social media, correct? Simply respond "no" to whatever it is. Get rid of the inconvenience and interruption. You can restrict access to specific websites if necessary. Set your devices to "Away" or

"Do Not Disturb" status. Stop wasting time and take command of your workstation in order to accomplish more in the time you have available.

When we experience unpleasant emotions such as tedium, dissatisfaction, or lack of interest, we frequently use distraction and disruption as a crutch. These responses are learned and habitual, but they can be overcome and redirected by practicing effective time management rather than giving up when the going gets difficult.

Chapter 10: Consider The Consequences Of Procrastination

Our senses may indicate that procrastination will protect us. Yet, we recognize that we frequently have a more negative view of ourselves after we've spent considerable time on a project.

When you need to postpone a task in the future, grab a pen and paper. Create a list of potential outcomes in the event that you delay. Then, formulate a plan for what will transpire if you do not delay. Consider the emotions associated with each option and record them on paper.

Consider your rundowns. By calculating the cost of delaying, you force your rational mind to weigh the benefits and drawbacks. Occasionally, you may unwittingly diminish your own chances of success. You may find mental predispositions or illogical convictions in your rundowns.

These beliefs serve as channels that mutilate reality. You may also experience a sense of danger or risk, which is normal. Your body must either stop, fight, or take off.

Recognize any signs of frailty and be aware of how you react to your depletion. However, ultimately you could determine which list appears legitimate (and performs the best).

Disengage

Certain individuals procrastinate because the assignment appears too large to even consider focusing on. Fixation and concentration are indispensable instruments for achieving our goals.

Attempt to disengage yourself as much as possible if you are prone to interruptions. For example, if you realize that emails and chats are distracting you or preventing you from completing your work, you can attempt freezing them. Or, if you had to view virtual entertainment instead of completing a household task, would you be brave enough to disengage from these distractions?

Compel yourself to devote a certain amount of time to a specific task. Set explicit termination times or design a workflow to accommodate this time frame. Identify small methods for isolating yourself from your interruptions. By detaching, you empower yourself to focus on the task at hand with greater probability. You are also putting yourself in a favorable position.

Employ a mentor.

It is essential to promote a safe and humane training relationship. Working one-on-one with a mentor can be of great assistance in combating procrastination.

Regarding any fundamental self-beliefs concerning procrastination, while working with your mentor, you should be undefended and honest. For instance, if you're nervous about having a difficult conversation with a colleague, ask your mentor for assistance with managing "the why." You may feel as though you are exposing yourself to risk. You may feel as though you are examining your functional relationship.

During these times, rely on your mentor to guide you through your perspectives. Your mentor can provide nuanced direction and patience. They will provide methods for enhancing your confidence while fostering accountability.

You and your mentor can work together to build trust, compatibility, and assurance. Together, you will make progress toward establishing a climate of mutual protection. Together, you and your mentor will formulate objectives that will achieve the desired outcome.

The five stages of overcoming delaying

As with any transformation, overcoming hesitancy can occur in stages. I have outlined five phases of overcoming procrastination and what you can do about them.

Adjust.

In this stage, you are profoundly present in order to perceive what is actually occurring. Consider carefully the major drivers and signs you may encounter. Maintain discretion and attempt to create a secure, consolidated space for your thoughts.

Mindfulness.

In this phase, you develop an awareness of delaying. This is a level of intelligence. In the mindfulness stage, it is essential to pay close attention and inquire about your default patterns. By recognizing your competitors, you will be better prepared to defeat them.

Recognize.

During this phase, you examine your attunement and mindfulness. This requires weighing benefits and drawbacks. Suppose, for instance, that you compiled a list of what would and would not occur if you procrastinated.

Consider the results of your actions (or inactions).

Thus, you are one step closer to conquering fear. Analyze this stage with care and self-awareness. You can reach an informed conclusion about your propensity for procrastination with the appropriate assistance.

Acknowledge.

In this phase, you accept the actuality of your tendencies. During this phase of acknowledgment, you may feel focused on. Alternately, you may sense a few shivers of disapproval. To truly reach the stage of acknowledgment, however, you must assume responsibility for default designs. It is exciting to make a significant decision to relocate and reevaluate your behavior.

Last but certainly not least, this stage involves taking action. Ideally, at this stage, you have made a decision. You are inclined to engage in physical activity. You've likely accepted a responsibility, and as a result, you're increasing your own assurance.

You are also undertaking responsibility for completing your tasks within a predetermined time limit. Consider collaborating with your mentor or making do

Chapter 11: Compile A List Of Your Daily Duties

A daily task list that serves as a schedule for the day may be the most efficient time management aid. Effective time managers schedule their days and complete duties from a list. Effective CEOs set aside time each morning to create a to-do list, just as pilots do prior to every flight. The ideal time to make a list is the night before, so that your subconscious mind can work on it while you sleep. You will frequently have inspiration and insights as soon as you awaken, allowing you to accomplish some of the most important goals on your list. Planning for the next day should be your last daily action. According to 49 of the most productive business executives, a simple pad of paper on which they jotted down everything they needed to do before beginning was the greatest time management strategy they had ever discovered.

Better Sleep

Many people stir and turn at night in an attempt to recall the tasks they must complete the following day. Before you go to bed, create a list of everything you have planned for the following workday. You will sleep much better and wake up feeling more refreshed. According to experts in time management, it takes approximately twelve minutes per day to write down your daily responsibilities. However, the time you will save by using this list will result in a tenfold increase in productivity. Twelve minutes spent on a daily list will result in 120 minutes, or two hours, of increased productivity once you begin working. This is a remarkable outcome for so little effort.

The ABCDE Methodology

After creating a summary of everything you want to accomplish the following day, group your tasks using the ABCDE method. In time management, the central idea is consequences. It is crucial depending on the probable outcomes of performing or not performing a task. When establishing priorities, you always begin with the task that will have the most significant impact. The ABCDE method is extremely beneficial in this circumstance.

Create a list of everything you need to do to get begun the following day. Then, before beginning work, assign each item on your list an A, B, C, D, or E.

An object with a checkmark must be completed. It is essential, and its completion or absence has significant repercussions. The obligations-related duties and activities that must be completed during the day are denoted with an A. You should act on the products labeled B. B tasks are less important than A tasks, but there are still moderate consequences for completing (or failing to complete) them. You must always complete an A task before commencing a B activity, per the rules. While C activities are pleasant to engage in, they have no lasting effects, whether positive or negative. Even though they are beneficial and frequently entertaining and enjoyable, activities such as chatting with colleagues, getting an extra cup of coffee, and checking your email have no bearing on your job performance.

Destruction of Time Waste Careers

Robert Half International estimates that up to fifty percent of working time is spent on C activities or duties that are irrelevant to the business. Everyone is a creature of habit. Successful individuals cultivate good routines and make them their masters. Ineffective individuals unwittingly adopt destructive behaviors that come to dominate their lives.

Many individuals arrive at work and immediately engage in time-wasting, futile, or unproductive activities. They begin their day by speaking with someone as soon as they arrive, reading the newspaper, checking their email, drinking coffee, and generally coasting through the day. However, everything repeated frequently becomes a habit very rapidly. Sadly, the overwhelming majority of employees today have developed the bad habit of wasting the majority of their time on activities that do not advance their careers or businesses. Stop permitting this to occur to you.

Delegate everything that can be

In accordance with the ABCDE system, a D action is one that can be delegated to another person. The rule is to delegate as much as possible to others so that you can devote more time to your A activities. Your A activities and how well you complete them have a significant impact on the progression of your career. You must promptly discontinue all electronic activities. In any case, you will never be able to effectively manage your time if you continue to engage in activities that are no longer necessary. People naturally and frequently slip into comfort zones as their careers and jobs advance. They become accustomed to performing particular duties in a specific manner. Even after being promoted to a position with greater responsibilities, they frequently return to performing tasks that are no longer necessary or that others could perform just as well or better.

Consider what would occur if you did not engage in this activity at all. If it has little to no impact on your business or career, it is a prime candidate for deletion.

Plan Your Work and Implement Your Strategy

Never attempt anything that is not on your agenda. Before beginning a new project or assignment, add it to your list and assign it a priority. If you do not record new activities and ideas but instead react to the constant demands on your time, you will rapidly lose control of your day and spend the majority of it on low- or no-value activities. Any type of time management strategy is preferable to none. Numerous smartphone applications are available for time management. On your computer, you could install time-management software. You could utilize a written, portable, and periodically updated time management plan.

Remember that the only commodity you can sell in the workplace is your time. Ensure that you are devoting the majority of your time to the company-building activities.

The Do Not Perform List

A not-to-do list is equally essential for keeping you on track as a to-do list is for completing tasks. These are actions that you decide in advance not to take, regardless of how tempting they may seem at the time. As Nancy Reagan once advised, just say no. Simply decline any engagement that does not represent your utmost priority use of time.

No is the most efficient word in the sphere of time management. Furthermore, this word becomes easier to pronounce the more you use it. People are the most significant time wasters, so bear this in mind. Consider whether it would be the most efficient use of your time when someone asks you to do something for them or assist them in any way. If the answer is no, you can politely respond, "Well, thank you for asking." I'll think about it and then consult my calendar. If I am able to assist you, I will let you know when I respond. You can delay twenty-four hours, then contact the person to let them know that you are now overburdened with work and deadlines and cannot assist. When someone asks for your assistance, say thank you and maybe next time. There will be space in your agenda.

Remember that you can only effectively manage your time if you stop engaging in unimportant activities. As the saying goes, your dancing card is already filled. You already have an excessive amount of work to complete. You will never complete the tasks and responsibilities you already have, let alone the new ones that arrive every day. Instead, he merely declined. Repeat it out loud and often. In no time, you will have complete control over how you spend your time.

Chapter 12: Time Administration And Its Significance

Calling time management "the core of existence" is a bold assertion, but it is largely accurate. There is no way to undervalue the value of time because time equals money. The central message is that planning and adhering to a schedule are essential for achieving success in life. Successful time management is crucial to your success and will provide you with all of life's benefits.

1.1 What is the definition of time management?

Time management is the process of controlling your time so that it can be allocated to various duties. When you do it correctly, you will discover that when time is limited and expectations are high, you work smarter, not harder, to complete tasks much faster.

Create a comprehensive daily schedule. Create a behavioral intention or "to-do list." List the essential tasks that must be completed on a given day along with the total quantity of time available for each task. Prioritize duties by importance, beginning with those that require the most attention and working your way down. Finish every unresolved task one by one. Do not initiate a new task before completing the previous one. Notate which tasks you have already completed. Ensure that you complete the duties within the allotted time.

Create a schedule for yourself and exert the necessary effort to adhere to it. Never wait for your supervisor to ask you a query. Learn to assume responsibility for your work. You are the person most capable of setting deadlines effectively.

Develop the discipline of acting appropriately and at the appropriate time. Work completed at the incorrect time is useless. Spending a day on a task that can be completed in an hour or less is inefficient. Reserve time for personal communications or check Twitter and Facebook for updates. Humans, after all, are not machines. It is difficult to remember every detail of the day, particularly when there are numerous distractions. Our parents and teachers have instilled this lesson into us from a young age.

Time is a valuable commodity. In the fast-paced, fiercely competitive business world of today, it is more valuable than currency. Money can always be acquired, but time cannot. Ensure that you focus on the things that are most significant to you. Time management is the active use of time to complete project-related duties and activities. For effective time management, every project activity must be planned, monitored, and managed.

Have you ever longed for more hours in the day? Do you often find it difficult, if not impossible, to complete all of your tasks and activities within 24 hours? Then, like most people, you likely believe that mastering time management would allow you to avoid the frenzied rush to meet deadlines, complete tasks without rushing, and have a great deal of extra time to devote to activities you have always desired.

This viewpoint is unquestionably accurate. Before implementing any of the pressure strategies recommended by all-knowing efficiency experts, it would be beneficial to have a firm grasp of the fundamentals. The pillars of efficient time management are command and equilibrium. In addition, scheduling your duties and objectives and managing your performance allows you to maximize the time you have available.

If you follow this procedure from start to end, you will have a comprehensive understanding of the scope of your work and will know how much time to allocate to each activity. This will help you allocate your time more efficiently across various responsibilities. Additionally, your time management skills will improve.

Chapter 13: Determine Which Portion Of The Elephant Appears Most Appetizing

So, you now have perfectly seasoned and cooked elephant steaks. But now comes the next conundrum: which do you consume first? Do you start with the delicate filet and work your way up to the tough hide? Or should you begin with the least desirable cut and finish with the most desirable? Or, you could combine soft and difficult steaks by consuming the toughest steak first, followed by the softest, and so on.

I am confident that you now comprehend the metaphor. Now that you've broken down your duties into their simplest and most manageable forms, you'll need to determine the sequence in which you'll complete them.

Obviously, the order of operations varies from case to case, and the decision ultimately rests with you, as there are a multitude of variables to consider. You may have to deal with a variety of factors, but let's examine two of the most prevalent:

Deadlines

This is likely the most prevalent factor. Tomorrow is the deadline for a 5,000-word essay, but you're also planning your sister's bachelorette party, which is a month away. Both are extremely essential to you for different reasons, but their due dates are quite distinct.

In this metaphorical scenario, the answer to which task you will complete first is fairly straightforward, but in the real world, you are likely to encounter situations that require you to think thoroughly and plan your tasks in the most efficient manner.

Importance

The significance of a task, as well as how it will affect your job or you personally, comes next. Even without a specific deadline, some tasks will be more essential and urgent to complete than others.

When it comes to work-related duties, it is generally advisable to prioritize the most challenging aspects of the job and leave the easier tasks for later. Alternatively, you could ease your way into a large task gradually by beginning with the simpler tasks. In general, however, it is preferable to dive in headfirst—after planning everything, of course. That way, you won't have the final boss constantly hovering over your head.

It may not sound appealing to begin with something challenging, but think of it as getting the unpleasant things out of the way so you can get to the enjoyable portions more quickly. Similar to how children—and, truth be told, some adults—save their favorite part of a meal for the end, so that they can savor the last few mouthfuls in peace.

When it comes to personal matters, such as home maintenance or even self-maintenance, it all depends on what you consider to be the most essential. Before deciding whether to paint the living room or the baby's room first, you must consider the advantages and disadvantages of each option.

Having said that, let's continue our house cleansing journey with the second exercise.

Exercise #2: Prioritize

Consider the significance of each of your intermediate objectives.

List them in ascending order of importance.

Consider the significance of each of your near-term objectives.

Also list them in order of importance.

(Optional) Purify your plan.

Don't be fooled by the apparent simplicity of this task; you'll need to do a lot of pondering and possibly even some compromising. Let's get into it.

Consider the significance of each of your intermediate objectives

Examine the long- and medium-term objectives and determine which ones require immediate attention and which ones can wait. Even if everything is essential, you will unfortunately have to make some sacrifices.

Decide which room in the house you will clean first as an example. This choice could be based on whether you want to begin with the cleanest (and therefore simplest) room, the messiest room, or your favorite room. It makes no difference which criteria you use to determine your starting point, so long as you have one.

After determining which room will be your top priority, you must choose the second, third, fourth, etc. Remember, for now, just concentrate on each chamber as a whole. We'll get into the specifics shortly.

List them in descending order of importance.

I did say earlier to write everything down, and I even provided evidence that it is beneficial! List the rooms or other midterm duties in the order in which you intend to complete them.

Consider the significance of each of your near-term objectives.

Now that you have established your initial level of prioritization, you can do the same for your short-term objectives. Place these minor tasks in the order that is most logical, most efficient, or the order in which you wish to complete them.

If you've decided to clean the living room first, it only makes sense to gather up any debris on the floor before sweeping or mopping. Likewise, you will not attempt to dust the coffee table if there are still papers or beverages on it.

Also list them in order of importance.

As with the intermediate objectives, writing it down will make things simpler. You could choose to use this method for the first midterm objective, plan and document everything, execute the goal, and then plan the next one. Alternately, you could plan everything at once so that you have a more comprehensive understanding of what you will be doing over the next few hours, days, or weeks.

(Optional) Purify your plan

If you're anything like me, establishing priorities and planning everything can leave your page or document looking a bit disorganized. It is a small task, but organizing your organizational plan can also have a positive psychological influence. Utilize subheadings, checkboxes, varying font sizes, and spaces to make everything more comprehensible. You could even use a mind map with your mid-term objective in the center and your short- and even shorter-term objectives affixed to it.

If your plan is orderly and organized, or even well-designed or attractive, it will be simpler to follow. Comparable to attempting to work in a filthy, dingy, and cluttered environment as opposed to a clean, bright, and hospitable one. This is an optional procedure, but I strongly advise taking it.

Regardless of the method you choose, you now have a game plan. You are now aware of precisely what you must do, the next step you must take, etc.

If you keep whittling away at these short-term goals, in no time you'll have completed a mid-term goal, followed by the previously overwhelming long-term objective. It boils down to organization and preparation. You'll discover that the energy you may have been squandering on overthinking can be used to complete the task and bring you one step closer to your objective.

I hope that has sufficiently pumped you up and inspired you to immediately begin setting and achieving objectives, but there's something else I'd like to discuss: What if the elephant is simply too large for one person to eat in time?

Decreased welfare

People's well-being and contentment can be diminished by procrastination, which can cause them to experience negative emotions such as guilt, shame, frustration, and sadness.

In one survey, 94% of respondents indicated that procrastination has a negative impact on their satisfaction, and 18% indicated that this impact is extremely negative. Similarly, when asked how they felt after procrastinating, over 80 percent of student responses were negative.

Mental and physical health decline

Procrastination is linked to a variety of mental health issues, such as tension, as well as physical health issues, such as an increase in the incidence of illness.

Additionally, procrastination is associated with difficulties in adapting to and appropriately managing health conditions. This may result in a variety of issues, including poor behaviors (e.g., regarding nutrition and self-care) and a lack of adherence to necessary monitoring and treatment.

In addition, particular categories of procrastination are associated with particular types of health problems. For instance, bedtime procrastination, which entails unduly delaying bedtime preparations, is associated with issues such as lack of sleep and redoubled fatigue.

Additionally, procrastination is associated with a number of disorders, including depression and insomnia; however, it is uncertain whether these associations are reciprocal or not.

It is unclear whether procrastination directly contributes to these issues.

Delay in acquiring permits

Not only does procrastination contribute to a variety of problems, but it is also associated with a tendency to delay getting help for those problems, such as when it comes to seeking treatment for mental and physical health issues.

In addition, procrastinators may delay or avoid alternative behaviors that could assist them in resolving their problems, such as not exercising despite the fact that doing so could help them feel mentally and physically better.

Increased procrastination in the future

Procrastination can, in multiple ways, result in a redoubling of the probability of future procrastination, resulting in a pernicious cycle of self-perpetuating procrastination.

For instance, hourly procrastination typically results in a lack of sleep, which can lead to diminished self-regulation and, as a result, increased procrastination, which can lead to a lack of sleep, etc.

Similarly, if a person repeatedly procrastinates on a specific task due to anxiety, they may become more anxious about completing it, which increases the likelihood that they will procrastinate on the task and related tasks in the future.

How to Conquer Anticipation

As with most other habits, procrastination can be surmounted. Follow the steps below to help you get started and avoid procrastination:

First, recognize that you are procrastinating.
You may be putting off completing a task because you had to reorder your priorities. Essentially, you are not procrastinating if you are deferring an important task for a reason that is truly intelligent. If you begin to put things off indefinitely or change your focus to avoid doing something, you are almost certainly procrastinating.
You may even be engaging in procrastination if:
Fill your day with duties of low importance.
Leave the essential item on your interruption list for a considerable time.

Multiple times, without making a decision about what to do with the e-mails.

Start a high-priority task and then quickly make coffee.

Fill some of your time with trivial tasks that others assign to you, as opposed to completing the essential tasks already on your list.

Wait until you are in the "right mood" or at the "right time" to begin a task.

Chapter 14: Consider Why You Are Delaying Actions

Before you can begin to address your procrastination, you must first identify the underlying causes.

For instance, are you avoiding a particular task because you find it tedious or unpleasant? If so, take measures to eliminate it as soon as possible so you can focus on the aspects of your job that you find most enjoyable.

Ineffective organization can lead to procrastination. Successfully organized individuals overcome procrastination by utilizing prioritized To-Do Lists and creating effective schedules. These tools allow you to prioritize and schedule your duties.

Even if you are well-organized, you may still feel overwhelmed by a task. Perhaps you have doubts about your ability and are anxious about failing, so you put it off and seek solace in tasks you are confident you can complete.

Some individuals worry about achievement as much as failure. They believe that success will cause them to be inundated with requests for numerous duties.

Surprisingly, perfectionists are frequently tardy. Frequently, they would rather escape a task for which they do not believe they have the necessary skills than be intimately imperfect.

Another significant cause of procrastination is poor decision-making. If you cannot resolve what to do, you will likely delay taking action for fear of doing the wrong thing.

Adopt anti-procrastination techniques

It is possible that procrastination is a habit – a profoundly ingrained pattern of behavior. This indicates that you cannot likely destroy it overnight. Habits only cease to be habits when they are no longer practiced, so try as many of the below strategies as possible to give yourself the greatest chance of success.

Forgive yourself for your prior procrastination. Self-forgiveness reduces the likelihood of future procrastination, according to studies. Self-forgiveness also improves one's self-esteem.

Commit to the task at hand. Focus on doing rather than avoiding. Specify a time for the completion of the duties that you are compelled to perform. This may assist you in approaching your work with initiative.

⬜ Give yourself an incentive. Reward yourself with a treat if you complete a difficult assignment on time, such as a slice of cake or a low from your favorite coffee shop. And validate your notice regardless of how clever it may feel to complete things!

Request that someone observe your current status. Peer persuasion works! This is frequently the guiding principle of aid organizations. Self-monitoring can be accomplished with the assistance of an online tool such as Procreator if you have no one to consult.

Act as you proceed. Take care of tasks as they arise rather than accumulating them for the following day.

Rewrite your internal dialogue. The terms "need to" and "must" imply that you have no choice but to perform a particular action. This could lead to feelings of powerlessness and even self-sabotage. However, saying "I choose to" implies that you have a project and may make you feel more capable of handling your responsibilities.

Minimize interruptions. Close your email and social media accounts, and avoid sitting near the television while you work!

Make it a daily goal to "consume an elephant beetle" first thing! Start with the tasks that you recognize as being the least pleasurable. This may allow you to devote the remainder of the day to work that you enjoy immensely.

If you procrastinate, your potential may be limited and your career may suffer. It can even disrupt collaboration, lower morale, and lead to depression and unemployment. Therefore, it is crucial to take preventative measures.

The first step in overcoming procrastination is recognizing that it is occurring. Then, determine the reasons for your behavior and employ appropriate techniques to manage and overcome it.

Chapter 15: Maintain a List of Tasks

The author of Jump-Start Your Job Search, career expert Nancy Collamer, stated that worrying about how much you have to do and ruminating about it when you are not working is counterproductive and wastes time. Maintain a schedule of tasks and adhere to it. And be realistic about the time it will take to complete tasks; if you schedule an hour for a task that should take 30 minutes, you will only end up frustrated. Partner With Colleagues.

Delegating tasks (including assigning projects) is another time management strategy; since others are more familiar with your business than you are, why not let them focus on what they're excellent at? Additionally, working collaboratively strengthens relationships with colleagues. Try This One Strange Method: Try turning off all notifications on your phone or computer if you find yourself becoming distracted by personal e-mails or Facebook.

Turning off e-mail notifications alone can make a significant difference in your ability to focus on what's essential right now. Disable Distractions: This may seem obvious, but it warrants repeating: turn off social media and email notifications on your phone and computer. Turning off your e-mail notifications can make a significant difference in your ability to focus on what's essential right now.

Create a Schedule and Follow It: Regardless of whether you use a traditional calendar or Google Calendar, it is essential to schedule specific times each day for specific duties. The objective is for you to be able to work more efficiently by blocking off specific periods of time during which you will be uninterrupted. Assess Your Situation: Several years ago, when I first began writing professionally, I was utterly overwhelmed because I had no idea where to begin.

Initially, I attempted to research every aspect of my new position as if I were returning to school for a master's degree! Then, I had an epiphany: Instead of attempting to learn everything at once, I decided to first determine what was expected of me. So instead of researching everything under the sun, I sat down and compiled an exhaustive list of my job responsibilities. Once I did that, everything else became simpler to manage because I knew precisely what needed to be done next and, more importantly, which tasks fell under my purview! Create a Done List from a To Do List: To-do lists can rapidly become overwhelming for many individuals. There is always something new to add to them, and you never know which tasks must be completed promptly.

To resolve this issue, simply add a completed column to your list. When you complete a task, note it off in this column. Seeing those checkmarks increase provides immediate gratification and motivates you to continue crossing items off your list. Utilize Timers for Focus Groups: Are you prone to distraction? Utilize timers when concentrating on a project or endeavor.

Chapter 16: Tips For Successful Time Management

Utilizing time effectively and working smarter, rather than harder, are the cornerstones of time management. It requires preparation followed by adherence to the preparation, which requires discipline.

According to the Pareto principle, also known as the 80/20 rule, 20% of effort produces 80% of results. This implies that only 20% of your accomplishments are significant, while the remaining 80% are irrelevant. Imagine what you could achieve if you focused more on the 20% of your efforts that really matter.

Therefore, we have compiled eleven suggestions to assist you workaholics maximize your time.

Establish precise objectives.
Your short-term and long-term objectives should be crystal clear, as they will help you determine what is essential and what is not. When you know where you want to go and what you want to achieve, only then can you determine precisely what must be done and in what order. Once you have defined your objectives, you can plan and organize a series of steps to achieve them.

2. Create a task schedule.
Your greatest friend is your to-do list. They can aid concentration, reduce tension and anxiety, and increase productivity by 20%.

Spend five to ten minutes in the morning organizing your day's activities, or better yet, create a list the night before.

List all your responsibilities on paper or on your computer. Focus on one task at a time after dividing large or complicated tasks into manageable, bite-sized portions that are not overwhelming or overwhelming. Crossing off items as you complete them provides a wonderful sense of accomplishment!

3. Set objectives.
There's a good chance you won't accomplish everything on your to-do list, so prioritize completing the most important duties. You must therefore determine which of the tasks on your schedule are truly the most important and urgent (which are not necessarily the same thing). The most important duties should be assigned a "A," followed by the next most important tasks with a "B," and so on. This will help you organize your responsibilities.

Create a schedule.

Create a daily and weekly schedule that includes time for vacations and unforeseen circumstances, using your to-do list and prioritization as a guide. Realistic schedules should account for interruptions and unanticipated events. Depending on the nature of your business, you must account for a certain quantity of buffer time.

If you have a schedule, you won't need to squander time and energy deciding what to do next; simply adhere to it.

5. Complete the assignment immediately.

Procrastination is a universal flaw, but for some it becomes a significant obstacle to success. You must accept reality and begin working on the impending report or assignment because you are aware that it will not disappear.

It is essential to examine the causes of your procrastination. Are you awaiting the "perfect" moment or disposition? Underestimate the quantity of time or difficulty necessary to complete the task? Do you fear failing (or succeeding)? Or have you simply developed a dreadful habit? Stop procrastinating and begin immediately, as the only way to eradicate a habit is to continuously act differently.

6. Manage your phone messages and email

Emails and phone interactions are frequently the greatest obstacles to effective time management. Unless absolutely necessary, avoid constant email notifications and let your phone go to voicemail; doing so can consume countless hours of your time and cause you to lose focus constantly.

You must provide yourself with extended stretches of uninterrupted time to concentrate on your task. To avoid constantly switching between tasks, you should only read and respond to emails in segments per day. It may be necessary to recondition others and their expectations of you in order for them to anticipate instantaneous responses as opposed to predetermined intervals.

7. Maintain a time journal

Maintain a record of your daily activities and the time they require. This will provide an accurate depiction of your time usage and disclose any interruptions. You may be surprised by the amount of time that is lost in ways that you are oblivious.

Throughout the day, monitor your vitality and concentration levels. This will assist you in determining when to perform various tasks throughout the day. You should schedule your most challenging tasks for times when you feel the most energized. For example, if you're most creative and focused in the morning, use that time to write or ruminate instead of responding to emails.

8. Pause frequently.

By taking pauses, you will keep your mind active and be able to concentrate more effectively when you return to your task. If you continue to work until the deadline, you will spend more time but produce less work.

Observe prescribed interval times. Try the Pomodoro technique to determine if it increases your productivity. Using this method of time management, you work in 25-minute segments (Pomodoros) with 5-minute breaks in between, as well as a longer break every four Pomodoros. Some individuals abide by this method for increasing their focus and productivity.

9. Develop efficient procedures

Invest some time in the initial configuration of your systems so that you do not have to stress about it later. Being organized and having efficient filing procedures for correspondence, electronic documents, and paper will save you countless hours over time.

Since you likely lack the time to do everything yourself, delegate less important tasks or responsibilities to someone else who is better suited to manage them.

10. Develop the habit of stating "no"
This is essential, as you have limited time and resources and therefore cannot say "yes" to every request. You must focus on the essentials and understand when to refuse anything.

Your career and work-life balance are dependent on your ability to maximize your time and discover new methods to accomplish more each day. Utilize our suggestions and observe your output soar!

www.ingramcontent.com/pod-product-compliance
Lightning Source LLC
Chambersburg PA
CBHW050251120526
44590CB00016B/2311